THE 5K CHALLENGE FOR SOLOPRENEURS

How To Make 5K in 21 Days through Social Media –

Without Spending Money on Ads

Joeri Billast

"Joeri is a genius when it comes to social media marketing. His book is absolutely a must-read for small business owners."
– FIONA HARROLD, World-renowned coach and bestselling author

"Joeri's book is a real, practical guideline which allows you to learn and take very useful steps, if you want to grow your business. A must read/have for every entrepreneur and definitely worth the effort to do all the exercises!"
– BIANCA SCHOONJANS – PhiNicka

"I can't believe the amount of value you provide for such a little investment."
– CHANTAL REMMERIE – Chan'Talk

"Very interesting book to improve your social media reach and to find the right customers for your business."
– DANA CYPERS

Table of Contents

DAY 1

Let's Begin!

Hooray! Today is the first Day of our Social Media Challenge!

I'm so excited about starting this journey with you and hearing about your success as you go through the challenge.

If you're struggling to get customers online, then this challenge will give you the clarity, process and support you need to make money on social media without having to spend money on ads.

Just remember, above all else, keep following the process.

Let's get started...

Before we dive into the specifics on getting customers, we need to do two things:

Step 1: We need to set accountability (so you get the result that you want).

Step 2: We've got to clarify your offer, so we know exactly where we're going.

STEP 1: Set accountability

This step is critical. Let me explain by using my own story as an example.

When I was struggling to get my first customer online, I had no following to speak of and no training on what to do to build one. I'd left my job in a large IT company as a business analytics consultant where I was helping businesses measure results and increase revenue.

I'd been there for five years and I had begun to feel stuck and trapped. I had also lost my mother around this time and it forced me to re-evaluate my life. I knew that I didn't want to spend another five years in the corporate world because I would never feel fulfilled or happy.

I had started to resent the fact that I worked so hard. I was helping other businesses reach their goals and was helping my employer make a lot of money and yet I wasn't seeing any reward for myself.

On November 25, 2005 I handed in my resignation and called my boss. I didn't have another job to go to and my girlfriend was 3 months pregnant!

My father was concerned. He called me and asked me if I was really sure. He pointed out I would be giving up a safe salary, holidays and sickness benefits. It was a real concern, especially now I had have a family to support.

There were no entrepreneurs in my family and my father had a successful and safe career for 40 years.

I secured a small contract that was enough to keep us going but it could have been cancelled at any time. I had to make my new business work or go back to a corporate career that really wasn't *me*.

People were depending on me and there was no job to go back to. I had burned my bridges.

I had to make this work.

And that's the point of this first step. If this is going to work for you, then you've got to make sure not getting your customer, not getting your sale, has got consequences for you. Yes, you are out of your comfort zone. And no, it may not feel safe but it's the best motivator to get it right. It's this accountability that will drive your forward and give you purpose.

So, here's what I want you to do: pick a date sometime between today and the next 21 days. That date is the day you will have your first paying customer. Write it down and mark it in your diary.

Next, choose a consequence for yourself that makes you really uncomfortable. For me, it was letting my family down, not being able to create the next stage of my life and having to find a new job to pay the bills.

What is it for you?

STEP 2: Clarify your offer

Now that we've got accountability in place, let's move on to who your client is and the result you're helping them get.

I call this your Ideal Customer Concept.

It's knowing who your customer is, the problem they want to have solved and the result you help them get.

If you already have an idea of your Ideal Customer Concept, that's great. If you don't, that's great too.

When it comes to knowing what you can help others with, I find the easiest and most authentic way is to offer something that you've personally learned through your own experience or education. This does not mean you have to be an expert on it or the world's best at it.

What I've realised after having worked with dozens of clients is that your core message usually stems from the messes you've overcome in your life. Put in another way...

YOUR MESS IS YOUR MESSAGE.

It usually revolves around one area of messiness or frustration in your life that you overcame.

For example, maybe you're like my client, Gregg, who wanted to help people to make good investments to give them a secure financial future. That stemmed from the struggle in his corporate career working for a big bank and not being able to truly help people because of the pressure to achieve sales. So, he started his own consultancy firm helping people to learn how to make the best investment decisions.

Grab your journal and answer these 4 questions.

1) What messes have I overcome in my life?

2) What were the lessons I learned from those messes?

3) What were the feelings you remember that surrounded that mess or messes?

4) What specific results did you get from overcoming those messes?

Set a timer for 10 minutes and just free write.

Don't edit yourself.

Don't filter yourself.

Just dump everything on the page and keep writing for the entire 10 minutes. This will trigger deeper ideas from your sub-conscious mind that will not come out if you start and stop.

So, to recap your assignments for today (and they should take you no more than 15 minutes).

1/ Pick a date between now and the next 21 days that you will have your new client by. Choose your uncomfortable consequence that will keep you accountable. Optional: send me an email via joeri@efficado.com and tell me the date and consequence.

2/ Write down your *Ideal Client Concept* - who your customer is, the problem they have ?-and the solution they will get with your help. Answer the **4** questions above during a 10 minute "no filter" brain dump session. Do not stop writing for 10 minutes.

DAY 2

Ideal Customer Problem

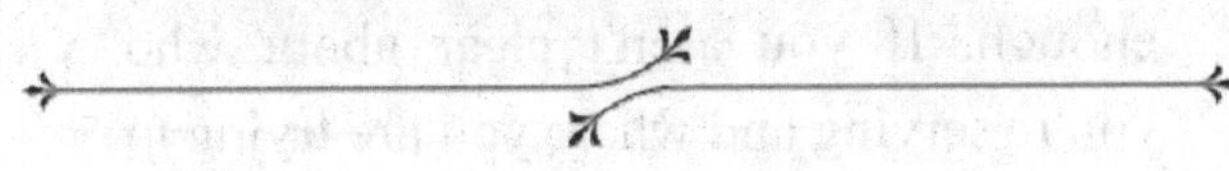

Yesterday we talked about your message being hidden inside of your messes. I had you answer 4 questions exploring the different messes in your life.

What stood out for you? What mess are you feeling most drawn to talk about? What do you want to help people with?

Grab your journal or open a document and spend 3 or 4 minutes answering those 3 questions.

Now that you have an idea of some of the obstacles you've overcome, we're going to put this together to identify EXACTLY *who* this offer is for.

The biggest problem I've seen with people who try and sell their services through social media is that they are not laser clear from the beginning as to who their offer is for. I cannot stress this enough. If you aren't clear about who you're serving and where you are trying to take them, your offer won't work.

Why is it so important to get clarity up front? Well, your clients choose to invest in getting help with you because they: *a) Have a problem* and *b) Trust you.*

Seriously. That's it.

This is why understanding your messes and how you overcame them is so important. That's where the trust part comes from - they trust that you understand *and* have a solution that works

On Day One we laid the groundwork to identify the problems that you've overcome so you can help someone else do the same.

Remember, your offer is a vehicle to help someone solve a problem they've had, and you are imparting your wisdom
and process because of what you've overcome. With that in mind, we're now moving to the main work for today.

I'm going to share with you one of the most powerful and deceptively simple frameworks for identifying who your ideal customer is and what they want from the offer, and why they want to buy it now.

Excited?

Good.

I call this the Ideal Customer Finder.

1/ Who have you worked with previously who has invested the most with you?

2/ Which client has referred others to you? This is your ideal client - and you want to attract more like them!

3/ What does your ideal client want more of - time, money or freedom?

4/ What is their biggest problem right now? What do they wake up worrying about?

5/ What pain or costs are they are experiencing with this problem?

Try to find at least 10 and list the top 3. Then choose number 1.

Let's go further and dig deeper. You need to get into the detail about your ideal client. Go to www.joeri.link/avatar to fill out my Client Avatar Sheet. This will ensure you are laser clear on your ideal client and remove any confusion.

Today's time commitment will be at least 30 minutes.

But do not skip this step. It is the most important step of this entire process. It will make everything that follows much simpler and easier.

To recap your assignment fortoday...

Spend 5 minutes brainstorming these 3 questions as you think about the messes you've overcome... **What stood out for you?**

What mess are you feeling most drawn to talk about?

What do you want to help people with?

And then jump into the Ideal Customer Finder and The Client Avatar Sheet.

Really spend some time with this task because this is going to lead us right into **creating your offer.**

DAY 3

Create Your Offer

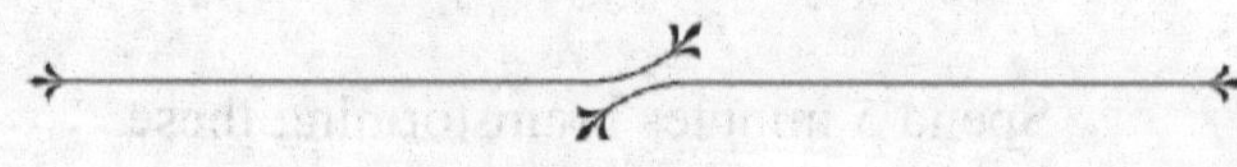

Today is the day!

We are going to create an irresistible offer that your ideal clients will love.

But, you must know first who your client is and what their biggest problem is. If you're not crystal clear, go back and review yesterday's chapter.

The main reason that stops people from being successful when selling their offer is a simple one: *it isn't relevant or isn't solving a vital problem for their client.*

At this point, it really is all about your client - not you.

It's not about what you like but about what your client needs.

I heard of someone recently who loved maps; beautiful books with geographical road maps. He thought they were wonderful and was sure he could sell lots of them. He had spent thousands of euros in buying stock.

I think you can guess what happened. Nothing.

No sales which meant big financial problems for him and his family. In today's world, people don't use maps. We have GPS, Google Maps, Waze and other easier ways to map our journey. His offer fell on deaf ears because it simply *wasn't solving a problem*

You cannot let an obsession overrule reality. You have to be in touch with the reality of your client's needs and what they are prepared to pay for.

When you get this right, people buy. In some cases, they queue all night to buy.

Let me give you some examples.

When I visited Lisbon 2 years ago, I went to the famous shop Pasteis de Belem where they sell delicious pasteis de nata. There was a big queue of tourists and locals wanting to taste the best pasteis de nata of Lisbon. Pasteis de Belem answered to a specific need: tourists who wanted to taste pasteis de nata and who wanted the whole, superior experience.

Another example was a morepersonal one. On July 23, 2010, I queued outside the Apple Store in Leuven in theearly morning to be the first in Belgium to own an iPad. The promise that Apple made with this new tech solved a specific problem for my business and opened up a world of possibilities for me.

An irresistible offer must have three components:

1/ It must solve a *specific* problem.

For instance, a photographer I know solves the problem of how to look professional and approachable on LinkedIn. He targets people who use LinkedIn and offers his photographic knowledge and expertise to solve a specific problem and as a consequence attracts people to him. He has found a specific gap in the market that he can fill using his skills.

2/ It must include a reason to buy *now*.

People are busy and need a reason to stop and take action. You need to give them a reason to buy now.

3/ It must be risk-free.

Make it easy for people to buy by removing the risk. Give them a simple money-back guarantee, so they don't have to overthink or hesitate too much.

Let's get into today's task and get into the details of crafting an irresistible offer.

I'm throwing in a FREE BONUS here. Go to <u>www.joeri.link/free-consult</u> and book in to speak with me or one of my team personally and let's answer any questions you have to keep you on track and moving forward.

DAY 4

Be Better

Today it's all about your competition…

Yesterday we worked on the creation of an irresistible offer but today we are going to check whether your offer is really different to that of the competition.

Our goal is to make the offer even better; to make it even more superior to anything your competition is offering.

Who is your competition?

Your competition is anyone who offers the same services as you. Your competition may even offer different services than you but if they get similar results, they are still your competition.

For example, if you wanted to lose weight you could hire a diet coach, a nutritionist or a sports coach. You could buy books that help you lose weight and eat healthily. They all aim to get the same results and provide solutions for the same problem.

Who do you need to look at? Look at the top 5 competitors in the area you are targeting.

How do you find out who your competition is? If you don't know them, use Google. When you search, focus on the keywords that make up your offer or the problem you are aiming to solve and see who comes up in the top 5.

Check out their websites. This is important as it will tell you who their target audience is. If they are serving the same audience as you, then pay attention to what they offer and the feedback they

are getting on their results. If they aren't serving the same audience then they are not one of you

Whyarewedoingthis? Youwanttofind GAPS.

You want to find a gap between what they are offering and what you are. These gaps are what you use in your marketing campaign to make sure your offer is even better.

This step is really important and it's your main task for today.

I've included a template to help you structure your research and complete your Competitor Analysis. Go to www.joeri.link/competitor.

Here are the main things to look for: grab your journal and make some notes.

1/ USP or Unique Selling Proposition – Do they offer something unique? Are there any unique benefits to using their product or service?

2/ Unique Mechanism – Do they have a unique way or method of working? For accountants for example working digitally is at this moment very appealing for their clients.

3/ Deliverables – What are you delivering? Are there any extras?

Going back to the example of the accountant. Do they just provide reports or, is there an analysis and visual representation of the information?

Maybe they even give advice on investments or how to reduce costs?

If you are a professional trainer, you can deliver audio files, online sessions, Q&A slots and perhaps, if your competition uses recorded training sessions, you can go live and interact more?

Ask yourself, can you deliver something special? Can you be better?

4/ Benefits - What do your competitors claim their clients get or what pain do they solve?

When you know this, think about whether you can offer a better benefit. If your competitors take away pain, could you do this too *but* make them feel even better?

5/ Price - What's the price and what are the terms your competitors are offering?

Don't just think about whether they are more expensive but look at the terms and conditions offered. Is it a monthly payment, do you pay before or after the service is provided?

You could offer a different solution. If your competitors offer a yearly fixed price could you offer monthly rates? Think about what will work and be as helpful as possible for your ideal client.

6/ What are the extras? - Are there any bonuses? Can you give extra value?

This is very important. When clients feel they have value for money they will trust you, recommend you and keep coming back.

When clients compare your offer with your competitors', are you giving them something extra? Maybe a bonus strategy call or a copy of your book? Or free access for an event?

7/ A guarantee or risk reversal? -If they buy something, can they be refunded if they are not completely satisfied?

What guarantees are the competition offering and can you do better?

So to recap - your tasks for today:

#1 Identify the top 3 or 5 competitors. Use a Google search if you don' t already know them.

#2 Check out their websites and social media - WHAT are they offering? HOW are they offering it and where are the GAPS?

Look at your offer - is it unique? Where can you fill the gaps and be better?

Happy researching!

DAY 5
Share Your Story

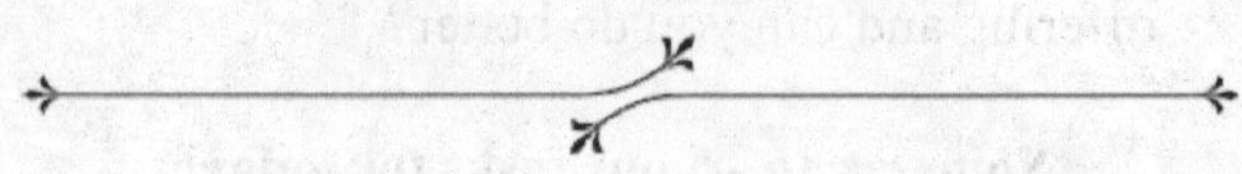

I'm excited about today because this is all about sharing your story or sharing *your why.*

Sharing your story is so important because it's crucial to start strong and to start by creating captivating content.

This is the point where you start to build trust and connection.

Your greatest challenge on Social Media is to GET PEOPLE'S ATTENTION. Don't forget you are competing with cats playing Chopin, dogs playing the drums and a stream of selfies from the gym.

Getting people to pay attention to you is your number one challenge and people love a story.

It's only when people pay attention to you that you can start building a following and start selling your products and services.

Offering captivating content is the only way to get attention, draw people to you, persuade them to like you, connect with you and, in time, to buy from you.

When you give content to people in a useful and generous way, you build a relationship that naturally leads to sales - whether it's buying your book, buying your services or buying your products.

When I was running events a few years ago, one of the biggest challenges I was facing was getting people to turn up on the day of the event.

Free events typically have a really low show up rate - sometimes only 30% or 50% - which means that you could lose a lot of money. Paying for the venue and having less people to sell to on the day itself can be devastating.

It's also very demoralising to present to a half empty room.

My show up rate was normally 80%, sometimes even 90% - more than double the industry average!

What did I do differently?

I provided good content to those who had registered but I provided this content in the days leading up to the event.

I created curiosity and an appetite for more.

The people showing up to the event felt connected to me and keen for more.

People are more likely to buy from you when you have taken the time to build a relationship with them. Connection through content leads to conversion and sales.

So, on to Your Story - your *personal story* or your *brand story*.

Let's take Virgin as an example. The Virgin brand identity is playful, modern and energetic. Everything about this company, from its advertising to its website, speaks of a truly universal brand. According to the social media manager for the Virgin branding team, Jill Fletcher, the company has one of the highest growth rates of all time on Facebook and Twitter - and this is just for the airline alone.

Regardless of where or how you interact with Virgin, you expect to see incredible customer service delivered with the same tone of voice, the same image, and the same unique personality that people love. Three words: playful, modern and energetic.

When I look at my own brand message, for me the three words are trustworthy, integrity and results.

So, ideally think of something which is unique in your industry.

Think of what three words you would like people to use about you and your brand and the words they would use if they were not in the room with you.

Think about three words that describe YOU.

These words will become your story - they will drive your content and all that follows your first post.

These three words are crucial.

Think about them carefully - write them down.

Next consider your language. We are looking for consistency and identity.

What is characteristic about the way you speak?

You convey your brand values by the way you act and how you dress but also by the way you talk. The way you speak and write is hugely important.

It's about the things you say and the way you say it; it's about the tone of voice you use when writing posts or delivering videos.

So my question is: is there anything about the way you talk, any words or phrases you use that people would recognise you by?

For example, when I do my LinkedIn Lives I always say "Yes! We are Live

again." Everyone knows that's me: it's always my first sentence and people know it and expect it.

Now, let's address the most important bit to cement your sense of identity and who you are for your clients.

You've already established what you believe, what you stand for and what identifies you

Finally, it's your WHY.

Write down the answers to these questions.

1/ Why do you do what you do?

2/ Why have you chosen the business, the sector, the job that you have?

3/ What experiences have you had that drive you?

4/ What do you know or have you seen that means you completely believe in what you are doing or offering?

I believe it is crucial to address this in your first video or post. It shows people your authentic self.

Sharing your story in this way also provides you with a plan for your next posts and videos.

It means you can create a **Content Calendar.**

Your story drives the content and means your content stays close to what you believe and what you stand for.

Your *Content Calendar* can start with Why and then move on to How and What - but I'11 come back to those later

So to recap our tasks for today - Day 5 of the 21 Day Challenge:

1/ Think of your three words

2/ Pin down what makes you unique, what's your brand?

3/ Make your WHY video or write your WHY post and get it out there!

For some of you that will feel a little out of your comfort zone but be brave and the results will speak for themselves.

Now for a really important bit of our journey.

We are aiming to do this REAL time and I have been guiding you, day by day, to keep you motivated, hold you accountable and create momentum to drive you forward.

But I know running a business, setting up a business, is hard so...

Take time to pause, reflect. Catch up and finish those tasks.

Go back to your notes and revise your thoughts - get really clear and ready to push on!

The next 2 days - days 6 and 7 - are for resting and catching up.

DAY 8

Connect With Others

Day 8 is about looking at the conversations you need to have with your audience but also with people who are not following you - *yet*.

So how does that work?

Connecting with people is everything!

In marketing there are three main stages:

Stage 1: Awareness – this is when people know you are there, they recognise you

<u>Stage 2: Engagement</u> - people start to like you, trust you and engage with you. They react to your posts and open your emails.

<u>Stage 3</u>: <u>Conversion</u> - people join your mailing lists, download from you or buy from you.

The question for today is: how do you CONNECT with people you don't know yet?

We've already looked at finding your ideal client and when using the following strategies, have that ideal client firmly fixed in your mind.

1/ Go into Facebook groups

Search for groups based on the products or services you will offer. For instance, if you sell wine, look at local sellers or artisan food and wine tasting groups. Or, if you offer advice on investments look at similar money advice groups.

It's not about selling directly at this point – what's important is engaging and starting conversations.

Respond and react to posts, offer gifts or links to helpful blogs or articles, ask questions... engage and build your presence within the group.

An ideal way to get engagement at this point is to offer a link to a so-called "lead magnet". You must not call it that, but it is offering something in exchange for a contact or email address.

A lead magnet used in this way could be: *5 Tips for choosing a Good Wine* or *How to Stay Healthy.*

You could also use a checklist – these are very popular. Checklists can be very appealing as people like to print things. It also means you can ask for an email address to send the downloadable version to, engage through Facebook messenger or share a link to your website.

This is the essence of engagement.

You are giving freely and building a connection.

You are generating an interest in you and your services and the people who engage now are potentially the people who will buy from you later.

It's not enough to just connect - you need to reach out and once there is a connection you need to nurture and build that relationship. You need to keep connecting and giving.

2/ Use LinkedIn to build connections

LinkedIn often feels more 'professional'. You can use a similar strategy to the one above and go into groups, but I would advise to use a tool within LinkedIn called *Sales Navigator*.

Sales Navigator has a lot of useful search filters. Use these to search for people who you know are your Ideal Client and follow up with them. That means engaging through their posts, when there is a profile update or good news is shared.

After you engage with them, you connect with them.

To initially connect with people, you can use the message service to explain why you are connecting and you can use information from their profile to make that link.

Once the connection is made, you can really reach out to them and nurture them - offer them a lead magnet or start a conversation.

There is one thing to keep in mind, especially with LinkedIn - connecting with people on LinkedIn is not just about collecting connections.

I gave an interview to Bloovi in which I explained that having connections on LinkedIn is not like having a collection of stamps to look at.

It's about doing something with those connections.

An extra tip: it's important to have a professional LinkedIn profile. When new connections look at your profile it should look like a mini-web site and not a CV. It needs to be very clear what services you are offering and WHY you are offering them (remember Day 5).

New connections will then know straight away why they should connect with you, what you will help them with and why they should get in touch with you. By the way, feel free to connect with me here: www.linkedin.com/in/joeribillast

3/ Be active on Clubhouse or similar social media apps

For entrepreneurs Clubhouse is ideal to give your business a boost and to be able to connect with a very diverse audience. The platform is open to everyone, both on iOS and Android.

Let me give you're a few guidelines.

When you've explored Clubhouse and feel ready to take the floor, start participating in smaller rooms. The chance that you get on stage is much more realistic in a smaller room. Larger rooms are interesting to learn, but the chance that you will actually get the floor is small because there are so many candidate speakers.

If you have the room's moderator's attention, so you can go on stage, try to make your point briefly. Don't be too wordy and try to keep the audience interested.

Have a clear profile picture that stands out. Among the often-numerous participants, it is important to stand out so that the moderator of the room notices you and calls you on stage.

Plan very carefully which rooms you want to follow. The offer is overwhelming, and you can spend a lot of time on it. You also receive constant invitations to follow rooms based on your interests, so some self-discipline to deal with this is not an unnecessary luxury.

Provide a clickable link to your Instagram and/or Twitter profile on your bio so that you can exchange messages with other participants after the room has ended and expand your network. NB: At the moment of writing, Clubhouse is adding a messaging functionality to its app, so have a look at this option too.

To recap - your actions for today, Day 8

1/ Look on Facebook for relevant groups - join those groups and ENGAGE!

2/ Search for LinkedIn groups and/or use Sales Navigator

3/ Use Clubhouse or a similar app to look for relevant clubs and rooms and make new connections through live conversations.

Share links and articles, give top tips and ideas, use a lead magnet and most of all nurture those new connections. You could pick either Facebook or LinkedIn or Clubhouse but, if you are feeling confident, combine different strategies. The emphasis is on connect, engage and nurture.

Whatever you do - do it profoundly and with the intention of building relationships.

Show people through your conversations that you are really interested in them and in helping them.

Go get talking!

DAY 9

Engage Personally With Your Own Following

Now you have followers.

You have a number of connections, new and old, and within those followers you will have your ideal clients.

So, now we need to talk about nurturing your existing connections, building conversations and drawing those ideal clients ever nearer to you.

Last week on Day 5 we talked about your **WHY**.

Your task was to create your 'why' video or initial post.

Today, on Day 9, we are looking at the **HOW** and your first task is to create your 'how' video or post.

In order to do this think about the following: **How do you work? How are you delivering your services? How is your way of working different to others?**

For example, an accountant could emphasise the types of meetings that work well; quarterly or monthly. They could highlight that their way of working is different because they send invoices via digital platforms or that their approach is personalised because there is a dedicated account manager especially matched to their client.

The 'how' video is also a way to continue the conversation. Because to stand out it's not just about captivating content but about starting a conversation and making people react.

Reaction is engagement. To stand out you have to be controversial. To stand out you have to be polarising but this doesn't mean you have to be shocking or rude.

You need to create a sense of authority; be clear about what you truly believe.

You can create this authority by maintaining absolutes. You don't have to be totally accurate to be an authority. Vagueness can be as effective as being direct when building a sense of authority.

For example, the American money expert, Dave Ramsay, says, "If you can' t pay cash, you can't afford it". This wording is an absolute.

What he says isn't necessarily accurate, and not everyone will agree, but it absolutely maintains the authority of his core beliefs.

Gary Vaynerchuk, also known as Gary Vee, is a very successful entrepreneur and internet personality and he uses the same authority building strategy when he says, "There has never been a better time in history right now to start your business."

He isn't specific about when that time is. Is now the best time to start a business? Or is he talking about 2016? Was that the best time to start a business?

This statement is an example of an absolute that supports Gary's brand of promoting entrepreneurship.

Your second task - Create an absolute statement.

Here are some words you could use to create your absolute statement: All, None, Always, Now, Never, Period, Guaranteed, I promise, Going to happen, Fact, Dumb, Stupid, Evil, Genius, Best, Greatest, Worst, One thing, Everything, Nothing, Everyone, No one.

Let's recap your tasks for today:

Task 1: Make a HOW video

Task 2: Create and plan posts on social media that are polarising; posts that shows what you feel, and are examples of what you absolutely believe. Do the same when you go on stage on Clubhouse.

Don't forget when you get a reaction, start the conversation and nurture those connections!

DAY 10

Seed The Need, Build Appetite!

Today we will talk about how to seed the need and how to build an appetite for your services.

Days 8 and 9 were all about connections - how to connect in groups, how to engage on a more personal level and about telling your story. Today we are looking at how to continue that nurturing.

We want to get people ready for your offer and for your launch so that they are more eager to buy.

A couple of things are very important:

1/ Give away your best content for free

Give away content in posts, announce you will be giving away top tips by going live, or invite people to download some free top tips.

Frank Kern is one of the world's most successful marketers and his most famous advice is to give away your best stuff: give people great content, content that is so good that they would pay for it.

It is tempting to think you could give away older material for free as if you are cleaning out your cupboards and giving away less valuable pieces to charity but that would be a huge mistake.

People will judge you on their first impression of you.

So, if your first contact with them consists of material which is dull and dated then you will be doing a lot of damage.

It may feel uncomfortable to give away your best bits but think of it this way...

"Metaphorically, if you have someone who's hungry and you give them a little bit of food, you've only whetted their appetite and they're going to be hungrier... " - Frank Kern

I recently did some interviews where I did just this. One was for the Flanders Chamber of Commerce magazine, 'Entrepreneurs where I talked about how to build your social media strategy, what is important and what are the elements for a good social media strategy.

I gave away some very useful content that I could have charged for but I decided to give it for free.

Another was for Bloovi, the online media website, about how to use LinkedIn

so that it's beneficial for your business. Again, I gave it away freely where others may have charged for the same information.

My colleague uses Instagram to post tips for online marketing and social media as part of the <u>effic</u>ado brand and there are some amazing insights and top tips.

Again all for free! Why?

Why would people buy from you if you give away your best stuff for free?

Because the people you connect with in this way will see what you give away so generously and expect the content they will be paying for to be even more amazing.

It's about trust - you have built their appetite for more

Use a lead magnet as part of the free content giveaway and that way you can collect an email address or contact so you can follow up and nurture them.

2/ Use visuals that seed the need and build an appetite

Use tools like Canva and Genially to make your content stand out.

The things to remember when using these are:

Pick a nice image: nothing which is too much of a stock image; an image with a relatable person would be a good option

Add some text - not too much and make it fit the media you are using whether that's Instagram or Facebook

Add your logo or try to use similar colours so that your images become personal to you and your brand and instantly recognisable

Remember these visuals are not a promotion but simply attractive images to BUILD APPETITE.

Ideally it would be an image which relates to the product, your service, or to you personally so you can build your connection with your followers.

In order to SEED THE NEED, you could choose something which is linked to the PAIN POINT: by this I mean the problem you are solving or the pain you are helping. For my followers that could be that they have a successful business but don't have the time or the confidence to build their social media profile. Images which reflect the problem or the solution reinforce the need for people to invest in your services and to trust your advice.

If you want to recap more about pain points go back and have a look at Day 2.

Actions for today:

1/ Look at what content you can give away for free: use visuals which reflect the need of your ideal client or give away information which builds an appetite for more.

2/ Go out of your comfort zone: use your posts to announce that you are going live on social media: on Facebook, LinkedIn, Clubhouse,... Say that you will be answering questions, defining your subject and sharing solutions to your ideal clients' main problems.

DAY 11

Go Live and Announce the Pre-Launch

Today, you are going to go out of your comfort zone and go live!

You made the announcement yesterday that you were going to go live and today it's about taking the leap.

A couple of things to remember:

1/ People love it when you are authentic – so don't worry if things don't go completely as you planned, just make sure you are not in a noisy environment.

2/ Not everyone will be watching you live
- a lot of people will watch the replay. Your video stays available on Facebook, LinkedIn and Twitter. On Instagram, you can **save the video to your phone's camera roll,** right after you've ended it. *And* you can repurpose it later.

Today I'm talking mainly about going Live on social media. I use StreamYard for my live videos on LinkedIn, Twitter, Facebook and YouTube but each platform has its own tools.

For Clubhouse I use a separate iPhone. Not only does this help me protect my time, but then I can use my regular iPhone to record myself when speaking in my rooms. I can then repurpose the result afterwards.

Why go Live?

You are going Live because you want to get leads. You can start getting your leads through email addresses.

There are three ways of collecting email addresses from Lives.

1/ Get people to comment and engage with your Live - plan the content of your Live so that it encourages people to ask questions, comment, react and engage. Ideally you want people to go from your Live to your website or to your lead magnet so that you have them on your mailing list.

For example, in your Live you would explain you are launching a new service or have an amazing offer coming up and ask if people want to be notified in advance. If they do, ask them to comment below or to send you a direct message.

It's an easy and simple way of collecting leads.

And - once you have these leads on your list you can nurture them! One tool I would recommend for this is ConvertKit

If you go to www.joeri.link/convertkit, you can get a free account for up to 1000 subscribers so you can tag people. I will go more into detail about tagging later but essentially people respond to emails with certain behaviours: they buy, click, open

or don't open. With a tool like ConvertKit you can tag these behaviours to create lists and email groups which help you target and build connections.

2/ Use Webinar tools like WebinarJam (go to www.joeri.link/webinarjam-free to get a 14 day free trial) **or Zoom.** The benefit of using a webinar is that people have to provide a name and an email address to sign up. As long as you made it clear yesterday that you were going live today you know in advance who has signed up..

As everything we've done so far has been around social media, I would advise to stick with going live on social media for now. However, this is definitely something you might want to consider for the future.

3/ When speaking on Clubhouse people, ask people to send you a direct message with their mail address.

Here's a few more tips about organising your own room on Clubhouse:

Consider organising your room with a partner. This is to avoid the "empty restaurant syndrome". Few people are inclined to enter an (almost) empty restaurant. Where there are more people you generate more interest.

Let people know regularly and repeat what the room is about and what has been discussed so far: on Clubhouse nothing will be recorded, so visitors who join your room a little later don't feel lost and can follow what's been said. It makes it more inviting, more engaging and stops you losing visitors.

What to talk about?

Yesterday we covered the notion of talking about pain points: stories about clients you helped and how they transformed with your help

The most important thing is for you to announce the launch of a service or product that will go even further in helping to solve their problem; something that will be even more beneficial than anything you can offer for free on this Live.

The call to action is vital: make it clear that if people are interested, if they want to know more, they should answer, respond and engage in the comments. You could ask them to send you a direct message and make it clear you want to give them the best service and nurture them personally.

It's not like throwing a plate of spaghetti against the wall and hoping it will stick - you need to respond to and thank people who take the time to comment and react.

Focus your message to the people that you interact with at this point as these are the people who will be interested in buying your services and need nurturing. They are your potential leads and your future clients that's why it's crucial to put in all the effort with them now.

To recap:

1/ Build your authenticity - show your authentic self; talk about what you do, how you help and 'give some free content by answering questions.

2/ Announce your pre-launch - share your excitement and create anticipation so that you get reactions and comments in order to generate leads. This is your pre-launch.

3/ Have a strong call to action - follow up on leads by asking people to connect via email or messages, your lead magnet or by leaving a number. Offer them early notifications or a chance to get on your mailing list for more great stuff - make it personal and make them feel special.

Tomorrow we will talk a bit more about the planning and preparation of the pre-launch itself and then next week we will be ready for the launch and... sales!

Good luck going live !

DAY 12

Plan and Prepare your Pre-Launch!

Today we need to go back to the offer we defined on Day 3 and launch it in beta.

It's important therefore today to check two things:

1/ Is your offer clear and practical? – does it make sense and is it appealing?

2/ Do all your systems work properly? – you have great offer and a service but can people actually buy it from you without any hassle?

For this step in your pre-launch you need a *sales page.*

I am going to go over a few systems you can use when you want to sell a digital or online product, or a physical product or service through online ordering.

Your sales page

A sales page, landing page or funnel all do the same job.

They sell the offer to your client and then create and collect leads and allow payments to be made to you and your business.

For your client - this is where you have whet the appetite of your clients, it's where your offer is described, where they can see the benefits, the features and read the testimonials. Most importantly it's where they can buy it!

For you - a sales page has to do two things:

1/ Give people the opportunity to buy from you and make easy, safe payments online that can be easily tracked.

2/ Collect buyer details to help you build your mailing list.

I use ThriveCart: it's easy to use and has a really simple way to integrate online payments. It's easily linked to PayPal or Stripe which most people feel confident using.

ClickFunnels or Kajabi are also popular. They both use Paypal and Stripe and also offer easy page building. For instance, you can add in extra pages like an, About Me page, Our Services or a Contact page.

We also use ThriveThemes. Why? It is an advanced, yet, simple-to-use

WordPress suite of website tools. It has truly conversion-optimized plugins and themes to give a real boost to your business. It ' s also cheaper than Clickfunnels or Kajabi.

I also use Convertbox, which is an automated on site email collection tool. It's purpose is to increase leads and sales through targeted engagement.

I think it is really important to keep a look out for new tools to aid your business and doing research , looking at reviews and trying new things is important.

Whatever sales page tool you use, it's important that it integrates with a mailing system.

This means you collect lead contacts and emails so that you can build a list and apply tags. It also means you can direct emails for upselling and avoid sending out duplicate offers to people who have already bought from you

This is why we use ConvertKit (Go to https://joeri.link/convertkit fora free trial) which I talked about yesterday. It's great because it monitors email engagement and behaviours which means you can tailor your marketing.

So, Day 12 tasks:

1/ Check and define your offer - make sure it's clear and attractive

2/ Create your sales page or funnel

3/ Tease people on social media - Keep building excitement and anticipation. Use engagement posts, like a behind the scenes post while you're creating your offer or a FOMO post (Fear Of Missing Out...) post. Mention on Clubhouse that you are working on something new that you're about to pre-launch.

4/ Send an email to all your leads - email anyone who connected with you through comments on your live yesterday or who engaged through your lead Magnet

The excitement is building!

The next 2 days if you are sticking to the schedule are for resting and catching up.

PS: At this moment in the challenge, people often feel stuck, because they need more time to master these tools. If you'd like my help to build your sales page, set-up a funnel and/or set-up the emails, reach out to me and we'll discuss the possibilities.

Just send me an email via joeri@efficado.com.

DAY 15

The Pre-Launch

Today is all about communicating to people that your offer is available and letting people know that your sales page or funnel is live!

Launches work best if anticipation has been built which is what we have been doing over the last few days. We seeded the need and built anticipation and today is the day we have been leading up to.

You will be telling everyone on your email list and everyone who has been following you and engaging with your posts or lead magnets.

The Announcement!

Announce your pre-launch offer via a post, video, audio, email. Ideally, you would use a combination of all of them!

As always, videos are good, but going Live means you can really show your enthusiasm and get immediate reactions which in turn builds even more excitement for your product or service. The same goes for stepping on stage in Clubhouse.

What goes into The Announcement?

1/ Share the opportunity - explain the product or service, describe what it is you are offering and why it's so important right now.

2/ Position yourself - people are buying from YOU, so explain why you believe in this as a solution or a service and how you know this will work.

3/ Build trust by teaching something or by delivering value - try giving one tip from your course so people are getting an idea of what they are getting and how it will help them.

4/ Deal with objections - you may already be aware of any common objections people may have or you could invite emails or reactions that you can answer.

5/ Demonstrate a transformation - give examples and share testimonials.

6/ Have a dear Call to Action - people need to be directed to your sales page and enter their email address so you can send them the link.

7/ Make an offer - You are in a prelaunch so make people feel special. Maybe they can get a discount or an offer for being here early? Offer a promo code that won't be available later. Build a sense of urgency or a sense of scarcity to encourage people to click before the date of the main launch, when these special discounts won't be available anymore.

Don't forget to use your other strategies!

Use your Lead Magnet. By this I mean your free calls, pdf downloads or top tip posts

Go back to them and make sure the offer and the details of the pre-launch are now attached to your lead magnets.

Use your free calls or strategy calls. These work really well with high-ticket offers. After a free call the potential client has spent valuable time with you, got to know you and has a sense of trust in who you are and how you work. To add your offer at this point is very effective. The idea that you are letting the selected few in on a pre-launch, cements the relationship even further and makes people feel really special.

Free PDF downloads, online presentations or videos also work.

Show your offer on the Thank You page when someone registers to get access. This again builds a relationship because not only have you given them something to help, but you are offering even more...

For example, I worked with a client of mine, a beauty salon whose lead magnet was a free 10% discount voucher. When they downloaded their offer, the Thank You page had a link to make an appointment so the voucher could be used straight away!

It made it easy, quick and encouraged direct bookings before the vouchers ran out.

Another tip if you only have a small email list or are planning a big launch is to consider a joint venture launch!

Go to someone you trust who has a big audience or email list and *'borrow'* the trust their audience has in them. Ask this person to promote you, recommend you and share your link. You then return the favour by promoting or sharing their product.

The final (pro) tip I have to share with you is to use the Facebook Ads Manager.

Put a Facebook pixel on your website using Google Tag Manager. It's not part of the *ads* in this challenge but it's something definitely worth considering. I want you to know it exists and I talk about it in my courses.

Using tools like this allows you to track the data for the people visiting your site which means you can re-target those people who exhibit certain behaviours on your website, blog or sales page but don' t necessarily buy or convert!

UPDATE 2022: Retargeting is not so effective anymore as it used to be, because people opt out to get tracked…

To recap your actions for today:

1/ Announce your offer and keep communicating with everyone on your lists, your followers and new leads.

2/ Make sure your lead magnets have a link to your sales page.

3/ Look at people in your environment and maybe **consider a joint venture launch.**

Go for it!

DAY 16

Make the Sale

For Day 16, it's a much shorter task but it's a very important one.

Yesterday we published the pre-launch; today is all about making the sale and focusing on the transformation people will get when they use your service or buy your product.

Tell them how their life or their business will change.

Tell them how their unsolvable problem will *finally* be solved.

Use a new email or post or go Live, but follow a similar structure to yesterday.

1/ First of all, thank people! For working with you, giving you their attention, following, commenting and engaging with you.

2/ Recap the offer or the launch, explain the opportunity.

3/ Recap your position - why do you believe in this? What experience do you have that gives you authority?

4/ Add social proof. By this I mean testimonials or a case study where you explain the problem and then the transformation; Before and After examples are often most effective.

Testimonials that work.

Photos and quotes are great, especially when the quotes are concrete. For example, 'I increased my turnover by 50% in the last 3 months - it's amazing or 'I've added 10 new clients to my list!

Video or live interview testimonials are also very effective. Be aware that you may be out of your comfort zone with these, but also the people you are asking to contribute might be too... So, help them out, name their product or business and give them exposure through your social media.

Ask people to post on Social Media. Just make sure you monitor them. You can also share existing comments from others on your social media. Obviously positive comments are best but you could also use a negative one and turn it around.

Put the testimonials on your posts, in emails, on your sales page, so you have consistent communication and are raising your authority.

DAY 17

Take Away Objections

Objections are the questions people have when they consider buying from you.

Common objections aren't always a NO.

They are often an opportunity to address misconceptions or worries a client may have that they just want reassurance about.

On Day 15 you might have collected or felt some objections. It might be that yesterday, on Day 16, people had questions or they responded to your pre-launch offer. Today is the day to deal with them!

The most common objections are:

1/ lack of budget

2/ lack of trust

3/ lack of need

4/ lack of urgency

How do you deal with them?

Communication!

You can use an email, social media post or a video. Again, stick with the structure from yesterday, but make it shorter. That way you are giving a consistent and reassuring message, but you are not just repeating yourself.

1/ Recap the opportunity- this addresses the lack of need in particular.

2/ Recap your position and what you believe - this addresses the lack of trust.

3/ Answer any questions you've had and take away objections - again you're building trust and giving information about budget and the need for your service.

You could structure this response as a FAQs post or video. One good thing about using a video is that you can transcribe it and put into an email.

It might also be useful to put some of the objections you've felt into a ranking.

First on the list would be the question or comment that comes up most.

You could also categorise objections. For example, if people have doubts about the content. Or about payments. Questions like, can I use different types of payment if I don't have PayPal? Can I get a refund? Are all common issues that people ask for clarity around.

You can also use these objections to define your Ideal Client - use the FAQ to suggest 'It's not for you if...'

It's best to have people who you know you will work well with, who will be positive, provide you with testimonials and be your ambassadors. It will help you to be able focus on your flow rather than draining energy.

Other things to do at this point:

Remind people of the transformation. Remind them of their NEED or the big change if they work with you or buy your product.

Add a countdown or a timer. This reminds people of the scarcity of what you're offering. We're dealing with a pre-launch which won't last forever! A lack of urgency can be an objection, so having a definite end point creates the feeling that they need to sign up quickly to avoid disappointment!

You could also reinforce your Call to Action - remind people of what they need to do and how easy it is. Simple phrases work best, for example, *go to the sales page, buy, click* or *sign up.*

To recap, today's action is to answer any objections and to keep communicating!

DAY 18

Post Purchase

It's very important that once you've sold something to keep building the relationship and to keep the momentum going.

There are some simple, next steps you can take to help to create a bond between you, your client and your service.

Your clients have already engaged with you through your free content, they've visited your site, had their free call or engaged with your lead magnet which has hopefully led them to buying from you.

Now, you have to sell to them again.

You have to *resell* what they have already bought.

Let me explain...

You want your clients to feel special and happy about your service or product and to keep talking about it. You want them to get addicted!

You want them to be eager to go to the next step.

One way to do this is to show results from other people like them that have bought from you. If it's a new product or service, you can revisit testimonials from other products or satisfied clients.

Testimonials are the best thing to convince people because they are real and they inspire trust.

You may be thinking if they've bought something already, why do you need this level of follow up? Why am I talking about selling again?

Because you want them to be *very happy. You* want your service to exceed all expectations.

You also want to reduce refunds.

The thing to focus on is Exceeding Expectations.

One way to exceed expectations is to give bonuses. Let me give you an example; if you were selling online videos or courses, the bonus could be a Q&A session or a discount on another course.

It's also good idea at this point - if your client is satisfied - to show them other products.

I call this *The Post Sale Value Offer*

Let's take the example of a coaching program.

When you are talking to a client who is happy with his purchase of a short course, you could offer him the VIP version or a longer, more targeted program and offer to reduce the price of the first course. You could tell them that the first course was for free!

This is a special offer or upsell. You are giving them the opportunity to take the next step with you and this way you can really offer value and help your clients even more

Next Steps - a recap:

1/ Check how the client is getting on implementing the service, using your product and send them a personal Thank You or a message saying how you are looking forward to working with them and getting to know them.

2/ Offer the next stage in the course or an upgrade - show new clients how other, existing and happy clients are benefitting from continuing or taking the next step with you.

3/ Tell a Friend - say that any recommendation leads to a bonus. When you have happy, engaged clients this is the time to get testimonials and ask them to recommend your service.

Whatever you do - keep the conversation going and continue to build the relationship.

DAY 19

Keep Selling!

Today is all about maximizing your future sales.

There are 5 things that are essential to help you continue building your sales:

Step 1 – Have a clear email marketing strategy

There are 2 types of emails that you need to focus on: broadcast emails for nurturing and conversion emails for selling.

Use weekly broadcast emails to continue to give useful, valuable content:

things like references to blogs you've written and top tips. In these emails, you are not selling but you can add links through images to take them to your sales page.

For example, if you offered 10 tips to lose weight, between tip 3 and 4 or tips 8 and 9 you add an image that people can click on to go to an online diet course.

This is an important stage in your email strategy because you need to add tags and this is where ConvertKit is helpful.

When they click a link to visit your sales page, you add the tag 'Sales page clicked'.

Then you can target your emails. This means you only send emails about the campaigns to people who have shown an interest in them. You can then add another tag 'In campaign so all the emails are focused on one thing.

These are your *conversion emails.*

So, ***broadcast emails*** are for people who are not in campaign and you want to nurture.

If they are in campaign, you are selling, so you need to send ***conversion emails.***

Ideally this is a series of 3 emails.

1/ Explain the product or service - maybe the client missed the pre-launch so you can use some of your previous content.

2/ Benefits and objections - go over the benefits and tackle the main objections.

3/ Position yourself and your product - use your testimonials, show the results and explain your point of view.

If they don't buy after these 3 emails, remove the tag and go back to broadcast emails.

However, if they did buy, add the tag 'Purchased and then look at another conversion sequence with an upsell. For example, send an email and say, *'you bought the 30-day package and I have a new and exclusive online course that would definitely benefit you too...'*

Step 2: Your email list (who do you send the emails to?)

Broadcast emails are sent to everyone who got your Lead Magnet. This is anyone who showed an interest and provided you with an email address.

Your Lead Magnet is the best way to build your list.

Make sure part of the download process to get free content is to leave an email address.

You should aim to have this part of the process automated so that when someone leaves an email address, they automatically have a tag added.

Having a strategy for email marketing is key to keep on selling!

Step 3: Webinars

Use a webinar to deliver valuable content that points back to a clear Call-to-Action, a link to your Lead Magnet or offer.

You can make this an Evergreen campaign, which means it is automated and you can just let it run.

Step 4: Work with affiliates

Affiliates are people that sell your products for you and get commission.

I already mentioned ConvertKit a few times.

And - because I like and recommend it, I have an affiliate link, which means that you get a good deal and I get the commission. Also other tools mentioned in this book have their affiliate link attached to them.

You could do something similar with your products and services. There is a simple way to set up the URL, so it's clear whose link the client followed and you can keep track.

Step 5: The Launch

Once the pre-launch period is over, follow the same principles and launch your product formally.

Continue building the excitement, stating how many people have already bought or subscribed and add any comments they have made. As soon as you have launched don't forget to start collecting testimonials and recommendations.

That brings us to the end!

Thank you so much - we have covered a lot and I hope I will see you in one of my courses.

Use the weekend (days 20 and 21) to relax and to process everything you have learned. In the meantime, if you have questions, get in touch.

Good luck and.......keep selling!

Joeri Billast

SOCIAL MEDIA STRATEGIST

About The
About

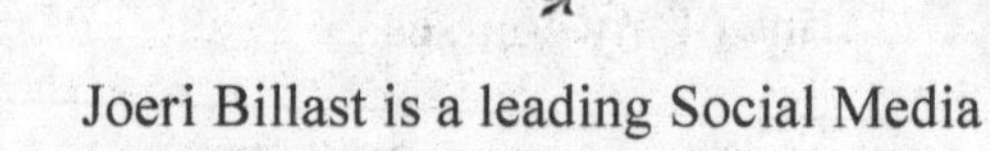

Joeri Billast is a leading Social Media Strategist.

He works with companies to build their business through social media.

Over the past 20 years he has worked in organizations and built his own business, selling it in 2013. The success of his company was the result of his social media strategies.

He now consults with entrepreneurs and organizations on how to use social media to build their business, increase sales and build a loyal customer base.

He has seen businesses struggle to get customers on social media even though they invest significantly. He is passionate about helping businesses understand the difference between having a presence on social media and making a profit.

He speaks around the world about Social Media for Business. He was featured on FOX, CBS and NBC and the cover of Manager Magazine, Entrepreneurs and Bloovi. He also has got his own 'Digital Comer' column in Perstablo Magazine.

Please Review This Book

Reviews help authors more than you might think. If you enjoyed this book, please consider leaving a review. It would be greatly appreciated.

Say Hello

You can connect with Joeri in a number of places:

Email: joeri@efficado.com

Clubhouse: @socialmediaceo

YouTube (ENG):

www.youtube.com/c/JoeriBillast

Facebook:

www.facebook.com/groups/solopre
neurmarketing

Twitter: @joeribillast

Instagram: @joeribillast

LinkedIn:
www.linkedin.com/in/joeribillast

TikTok:
www.tiktok.com/@efficado

Site: www.efficado.com

Blog(ENG): www.joeribillast.com

Blog (NL): www.joeribillast.be

Podcast: www.cmo-stories.com or find it
on your favourite podcast app